CHRISTINE BROWN

Bartók's Mikrokosmos

A GUIDE FOR PIANO TEACHERS

WITH AN INTRODUCTION
BY PETER BARTÓK

BOOSEY & HAWKES
LONDON

Boosey & Hawkes Music Publishers Limited
295 Regent Street, London W1R 8JH
and at
Paris, Bonn, Johannesburg, Sydney,
Tokyo, Toronto and New York

© Copyright 1988
by Boosey & Hawkes Music Publishers Limited,
London

Printed and published in the United Kingdom
First published 1988

All rights reserved.
No part of this publication may be reproduced, by photocopying
or other means, without the prior permission of the Publishers.

Typography and design by
Cinamon and Kitzinger
17 Willow Street, London EC2A 4QH

Printed in England by
Creative Colour Print, Watford

ISBN 0 85162 042 6

Acknowledgement:
The illustrations on pages 8, 13, 14 and 17 are reproduced from
Ferenc Bónis: *Béla Bartók: His Life in Pictures and Documents*,
Boosey & Hawkes, London, 1972, by courtesy of the author

Contents

Introduction by Peter Bartók 5

Bartók, Pianist, Teacher and Composer 7

Mikrokosmos 10

Folk Music 12

Modes and Tonality 15

Rhythm 18

A New Style of Technical Training 20

Pedalling 23

Development of Musicianship 23

A Textbook for Composers 24

Why use *Mikrokosmos*? 25

Publisher's Note 29

Christine Brown: Biographical Note 32

Introduction by Peter Bartók

Christine Brown's commentary so well illuminates the many-faceted nature of *Mikrokosmos* and its use in music-teaching 'from the very beginning'. Indeed, those who completed their 'journey through [my father's] "little world"' have been introduced along the way to a large variety of scales, rhythmic patterns, and to ensemble music-making. They have travelled a great distance, for the pieces in the last volume undoubtedly require the skills of an accomplished pianist. (I never progressed beyond the beginning stage, for my father and I became separated through circumstances such as his travel to the United States and his later illness.)

As a beginner, many of my tasks consisted of exercises. Not just scales, but more complex ones each designed to stress one specific problem. The little pieces he wrote – spontaneously at times during a lesson – also dealt with a certain particular feature in music. I did not know then, that some of these pieces and exercises would later become incorporated into an organized series of pieces to be called *Mikrokosmos*; nor could I have dreamed that some fifty years later I would be given the privilege of carefully examining all this music in the preparation of a definitive edition.

My father's study was the quietest room in the house where we last lived in Budapest. It was entered through double doors, one of which was heavily padded. This was the room where my father had his desk and his piano; this is where I received the few piano lessons from him.

In that quiet, isolated room, there were always flying insects! They consituted one disturbance my father did not seem to mind. At one of our lessons so many bugs circled around the lamp, and my head, that I could not maintain a serious composure – while my father did not seem to comprehend what went wrong with me. The flies were tolerated, sometimes gently ushered out of the window. Perhaps one of these served as the model for *From the Diary of a Fly*.

Peter Bartók

Bartók, Pianist, Teacher and Composer

Béla Bartók was born in Hungary in 1881. Both his parents were teachers. His father, director of an agricultural school and a keen amateur musician, died when Béla was only seven, so his mother resumed school teaching in order to support herself and her two children. Béla had received his first piano lessons from his mother on his fifth birthday, although even earlier he had been able to play as many as forty folk songs with one finger. He made his first concert appearance at the age of eleven, playing a movement from Beethoven's *Waldstein* sonata and one of his own compositions, *The Course of the Danube*. The following year he became a pupil of László Erkel in Pózsony, where he had the opportunity to take part regularly in chamber music, a valuable contribution to his musical education.

In 1899 Bartók entered the Academy of Music in Budapest, where he studied the piano with István Thomán, who himself had been a pupil of Liszt. Bartók later acknowledged with gratitude the debt he owed Thomán, not only for his fine piano teaching, but also because he took a paternal interest in the fatherless boy, lending him books, buying him music and inviting him to concerts. It was Thomán who recommended Bartók to the composition teacher Hans Koessler, little realising that eventually composition would take precedence over piano playing in Bartók's life. Thomán passed on to his pupil what he had learned of Liszt's technique, and Bartók's performance of Liszt's *Sonata in B Minor* at an Academy concert received unanimous praise.

On leaving the Academy in 1903 Bartók began to give concerts both at home and abroad, but only four years later he was appointed to succeed Thomán as professor in charge of the advanced course at the Academy of Music. Bartók admitted that he was not particularly attracted to teaching, but he accepted the post because it gave him the opportunity to settle down in Hungary and pursue the folk song research which had become his consuming interest. However, he undertook his professional duties with meticulous care and became a teacher much sought after by students from all over the world.

Photo: Alex Kertész

Bartók in his room at the Academy of Music in Budapest, 1927

Bartók was regarded by many of those who heard him as one of the greatest pianists of his time. From the evidence of recordings we can discern features of his playing – crisp fingering and clean articulation, clarity of chording, rhythmic energy, subtle use of *rubato*, an intense singing quality of tone (particularly noticeable in his playing of *Mikrokosmos* 94), marvellous grading of tone within a wide range of dynamics and, above all, a passionate response to the music. His repertoire was astonishingly wide, ranging from works by seventeenth century composers to those of his contemporaries.

One outcome of Bartók's post at the Academy was that he edited for teaching purposes a large amount of keyboard music, including what he entitled *The Well-Tempered*

Keyboard by Bach. This edition is of particular interest to piano teachers for the fingering, as Bartók indicates expansion and contraction from a five-finger position more often than the turning of the hand over the thumb or the turning of the thumb under the hand. This style of fingering is developed in *Mikrokosmos*, where the turning under of the thumb is not required until Volume 4.

Bartók's educational activities also gave rise to many compositions. The *Twenty Hungarian Folk Songs*, ten set by Bartók and ten by his friend Kodály, were first published in 1906 with the intention of making the general public aware of the existence of Hungarian folk music, still a living tradition among the peasants in remote areas. The purpose of *Ten Easy Pieces*, published in 1908, was to provide pianists with simple music in a contemporary style. The piano pieces entitled *For Children* were also published in 1908. Within necessary technical limitations, these arrangements of Hungarian and Slovakian folk songs furnish children with examples of their musical heritage, bridging the gap between classical and modern music and expanding the cultural horizons of the young pianist.

In 1912 Bartók and a colleague, Sándor Reschofsky, wrote a *Piano Method* in response to a commission. Included in the *Method* were eighteen pieces by Bartók, each designed to solve a particular technical or musical problem. The *Method* did not become widely used, but Bartók learned much from working on it, and many of the ideas were later expanded in *Mikrokosmos*.*

The *Forty-Four Duos* for violin were also written to a commission. The German violin pedagogue Dr Erich Doflein asked Bartók's permission to transcribe for violin duo some of the pieces from *For Children*, but Bartók rejected the idea, preferring to write original duos. All but two of the pieces are based on peasant melodies, and the duos are arranged in progressive order, with the players taking an equal share of the melody and the accompaniment. They foreshadow *Mikrokosmos* in the wide variety of structural and contrapuntal devices used, and in their abiding musical value.

* English edition, edited by Leslie Russell, published by Editio Musica Budapest 1968.

Both Bartók and Kodály were concerned to raise the standard of Hungarian musical education. They considered that for urban children, who, unlike the peasants, had no musical tradition, musical education must begin with choral singing. So Bartók wrote *Twenty-Seven Choruses* for two- and three-part children's voices. They are settings of his own texts and their melodies are in the style of peasant children's songs, with contrapuntal imitations. The melodies show Bartók's fondness for the tritone and the flattened seventh, features present in many of the pieces in *Mikrokosmos*.

Mikrokosmos is Bartók's finest pedagogical work. In it his ideas on piano teaching found their fullest expression. The skill of the mature composer and the analytical mind of the devoted teacher are put at the service of piano pupils, who are led, gently and methodically, from the simple eight-bar unison melody which opens the work to the complex *Dances in Bulgarian Rhythm* which conclude it.

Mikrokosmos

Mikrokosmos – 'Little World' – is a series of 153 pieces, arranged in six volumes. Written at the height of Bartók's career, between 1926 and 1939, the work was first published in 1940. The title is apt, for all the pieces are 'little' in the sense of being short. Only one lasts for longer than three minutes, most can be played in under two minutes and many in less that one minute. *Mikrokosmos* contains a world of different styles of piano music in miniature form – a little world of music for children and adults alike.

Bartók wrote the pieces in the first two volumes for Peter, his younger son, who began to learn the piano at the age of nine. Although circumstances forced Peter to give up his lessons, his father carried on writing until he had completed the concert-standard pieces in the sixth volume. Bartók frequently performed pieces from *Mikrokosmos* in his own recitals,* and in his farewell concert in Budapest before he

---

* In 1938 he included fifteen pieces in a recital given at the London showrooms of Boosey & Hawkes during the course of that year's ISCM Festival.

left Hungary for voluntary exile in America, he included no fewer than ten of them.

Mikrokosmos is not a 'piano method' in the traditional sense. As Bartók explains in his Preface, it should be used in conjunction with other material such as easy pieces by Bach and studies by Czerny. Technical and theoretical instruction are left to the teacher, apart from the exercises found in the appendix to each of the first four volumes. The exercises are designed to prepare the pupil for technical problems arising in the pieces and, as Bartók puts it, 'should be studied some time in advance of, and not immediately before, attempting to learn the pieces containing the related problems'.

In his scrupulously exact notation Bartók leaves nothing to chance. A perfectionist himself, he expects those who play his music to follow his detailed instructions with the utmost care and devotion.

In writing *Mikrokosmos* Bartók was following a tradition dating from Couperin's *Art of playing the harpsichord*. Bach's 'Notebooks' for his wife, Anna Magdalena, and his son, Wilhelm Friedemann still provide stimulating pieces for elementary keyboard players, while his *Clavierübung* demonstrates the full range of keyboard techniques of his time. Schumann's *Album for the Young* is much less systematic, but it contains valuable teaching material, particularly as there are so few pieces in a romantic style suitable for young players*.

Bartók once wrote, 'Only a fool would build in defiance of the past', so it is not surprising that in *Mikrokosmos* he pays a musical tribute to these three composers – to Bach in **79**, to Schumann in **80**, and, by implication, to Couperin in **117**.

Mikrokosmos provides an easily accessible means of studying Bartók's style for the 153 pieces reveal almost all his compositional techniques. Lacking only the larger forms, *Mikrokosmos* summarises Bartók's pianistic and compositional theories, his economy in utilizing thematic material, his masterly use of counterpoint, his individual harmonic idiom and the metrical fluidity of his melodies.

* This tradition has been continued by composers of a more recent generation, notably the Hungarian György Kurtág, whose four-volume work *Játékok* ('Games') develops the 'game aspect' of learning the piano through a series of progressive pieces (EMB / Boosey & Hawkes).

The texture of the pieces in *Mikrokosmos* shows how the luxuriant style of Bartók's early writing for the piano had become refined. The mature composer's desire for clarity and symmetry results in pieces of transparent texture.

Bartók's love of order and his meticulous attention to detail can be seen on every page of *Mikrokosmos*. He was always careful to provide exact instructions for performers of his works (the preface to the *Sonata for Two Pianos and Percussion* even includes a diagram of where the instruments shoud be placed in relationship to one another) and for each piece of *Mikrokosmos* he provides fingering, a metronome mark and its exact duration. For many pieces he used an Italian term to denote speed and mood, while for some the title provides an additional guide to interpretation.

Starting from the *Six Unison Melodies* in Volume 1 the pieces progress in difficulty. Some are designed to solve particular technical problems, others are more concerned with problems of style. Many pieces concentrate on particular devices. Some pieces (**51**, **63**, **107**, **142**) provide the opportunity to explore tone-colour in mood pictures influenced by the world of nature. Bartók was an enthusiastic collector of insects and was fascinated by the sounds they made. *Buzzing*, **63**, is both a marvellous sound picture and an excellent slow trill study. *From the Diary of a Fly*, **142**, tells the more dramatic story of a fly escaping from a spider's web. The desperate sound of the fly's buzz is depicted by *tremolando* chords in which the notes grow closer and closer together.

Folk Music

One of the most important influences on Bartók as a composer was his discovery of genuine Hungarian folk music. In his youth Bartók shared the assumption of Liszt and Brahms that Hungarian folk music was that of the gypsies, but in 1904 he heard a peasant girl, Lidi Dósa, singing a genuine folk melody, and soon recognised the decisive influence folk music was to have on his life's work. 'Folk music studies are as necessary to me as fresh air is to other people', he wrote, and he also claimed that the happiest

*Bartók
the Collector...
A water-colour
of Bartók
by his cousin
Ervin Voit
(reproduced by
kind permission of
Béla Bartók Jr.)*

days of his life were those he spent among the peasants, researching their music.

With his friend Kódaly, and later on his own, he travelled into the remote areas of Eastern Europe collecting songs and dance tunes and studying the folk instruments.

Bartók's interest in folk music was both scientific and creative, and occupied him from 1904 until his last illness in 1945, when he was still busy transcribing and classifying

Bartók on a folk-song collecting tour in Transylvania in 1907

Photo by István Kováts

Serbo-Croatian folk material for Columbia University. Speaking of Hungarian folk songs he said, 'I look upon them as tiny masterpieces, in the same way as I value a fugue by Bach or a Sonata by Mozart in the domain of more elaborate forms.' He particularly admired the concise, concentrated expression of a musical idea found in the songs, and freedom from the unessential became a feature of his own style.

Bartók declared in 1933 that his own music was influenced primarily by the folk music of Hungary, Slovakia and Rumania. He was later to find that not only were the nations of Central Europe inextricably bound together by their intertwined folk lore, but that traces of the same tunes could be found in the music of the Arabs, Turks and Asiatic peoples. Bartók regarded a folk song as a miniature masterpiece, perfect in form and with great expressive power.

As the short forms of folk music are particularly suitable for children, Bartók made much use of them in his educational works such as *For Children* and the violin *Duos*. *Mikrokosmos*, however, contains only a handful of folk melodies, but it is pervaded by the essence of folk music, for Bartók found that he had so assimilated the idiom that he was able to use it as his musical mother-tongue.

Modes and Tonality

Bartók discovered that the vast majority of the folk songs he collected were not in the major or minor keys with which we are most familiar, but in the old 'ecclesiastical' modes or the even older pentatonic mode. Each mode has a different order of tones and semitones, giving it a particular character.

Bartók early realised that folk music was an ideal starting point for what he called 'a musical renaissance'. In freeing himself from the limitations of the major/minor key system through his use of modes, pentatonic, whole-tone and self-devised scales he was able to widen the concept of tonality. Pieces from *Mikrokosmos* illustrate his procedures. Starting from traditional European classical tonality (**1**, **2a**, **2b**, **4**, **6**, **9**) modes are introduced (**5** Aeolian, **7** Phrygian, **3** Dorian, **11** Mixolydian, **24** Lydian). The chromatic scale

Chart of Scales and Modes in Mikrokosmos.

To assist comparison of their structures, the modal scales have been 'transposed', so that each has its 'final' on C. The piece-number references are not exhaustive.

appears for the first time in **54** and an 'Oriental style' G minor with a sharpened fourth in **58**. Bartók combines and contrasts F minor and the Lydian mode on F in **59**, while in **61** he combines a pentatonic melody with a Lydian mode accompaniment.

The Lydian mode, with its emphasis on the tritone, or augmented fourth, had a profound influence on Bartók's music. The augmented fourth divides the octave into two equal halves, and this symmetry appealed to the composer, who began to use the augmented fourth as a 'dominant', thus broadening the classical system of tonal relationships, previously based on the unequal division of the scale into a perfect fourth and a perfect fifth.

Bartók featured the whole-tone scale in **136** and bitonality in **70**, **86** and **99**. The final chords of **108**, **125** and **143** show the way in which the composer regarded a key not as exclusively major or minor, but as notes grouped round a tonal centre.

There are no pieces in *Mikrokosmos* without a tonal centre, although the title of **81**, *Wandering*, seems to suggest the lack of a fixed key. The music certainly wanders, touching all twelve notes of the chromatic scale, but it comes to rest finally on a G minor triad.

Bartók recording Slovak folk songs

Rhythm

The variety and complexity of the rhythms found in *Mikrokosmos* are a natural counterpart to the wide-ranging tonality of the pieces. Bartók himself had a remarkably strong rhythmic sense. His mother reported that she could not induce the small child to count, for he felt rhythms instinctively. Andor Földes, a former pupil, singled out Bartók's 'almost uncanny sense of rhythm' as the outstanding characteristic of his playing.

Keen rhythmic awareness is developed in those who study *Mikrokosmos*. Regard for the exact duration of notes and rests is a fundamental requirement from the beginning. The introduction of a rest on the first beat of a bar (**6**), syncopation through tied notes (**9**) and a change of metre (**12**) are a good indication of what is to follow. Pupils are led step by step to an understanding not only of many kinds of syncopation and changing metres, but also of unusual time signatures, irregular groupings of notes and cross rhythms.

The use in the same piece of even and uneven metres, a procedure stemming from folk music, is almost a fingerprint of Bartók's music, and it occurs as soon as **12**, for it is much better for pupils to meet changing metres early, before they come to regard them as difficult. Although there is no specific theoretical teaching in *Mikrokosmos*, the theoretical aspect of rhythm is not neglected. The difference between simple and compound time is beautifully illustrated in **32** and **33**, and pupils who study the pieces side by side will understand, and therefore remember, the distinction.

In **55** the use of triplet eighth-notes and pairs of eighth-notes in the same piece, firmly fixes their relationship in the minds of pupils, and although neither of the pianists in this two-piano duo has to perform two notes against three, they hear the effect of the cross-rhythm in the last three bars as simultaneously the first pianist plays triplets and the second pianist pairs of eighth notes. This is the sort of bonus that occurs frequently in teaching from *Mikrokosmos*.

Rhythmic problems are dealt with at various levels, not just introduced and assumed to have been mastered. Syncopation, for example, is introduced in a unison piece (**9**)

Mikrokosmos:
*Intermediate draft
showing* **32** *and* **33**
*(from the
Bartók Archive,
reproduced
by courtesy of
Peter Bartók)*

and then occurs again in **27**, where a note in the new independent left hand part takes the place of the foot-tap recommended in **9**. Unusual metres occur from **48**, and through studying **82**, **100**, **113** and **115**, pupils are prepared for the rhythmically complex pieces of the last two volumes, especially those in which the beats within the bar are of varying lengths.

This so-called Bulgarian rhythm occurs in much of Bartók's music, particularly in the Fifth String Quartet. One, or more than one, beat in each bar is lengthened by half, so ♫ becomes ♪♪♪ , a procedure which Bartók likened to a dynamic stress.* These rhythms came into being in village music-making and can best be appreciated by watching Bulgarian dancers.

A New Style of Technical Training

The emphasis on unison playing is a unique feature of *Mikrokosmos*, and pupils who study these pieces will develop an even touch and a rich quality of tone. The first six pieces are in unison, with the hands either one or two octaves apart, and there are more unison melodies from **18** to **21** when intervals larger than a second appear for the first time. Passages in unison occur in many other pieces, and in **137** the whole range of the keyboard is used in a rich and powerful exposition of unison writing.

The many pieces using parallel motion such as **11**, **16** and **62** are also useful for the development of tone. The hands must play with equal intensity and must be perfectly synchronised. To balance the tone between the hands the pupil must listen carefully, and listening will lead to musical, rather than mechanical, playing.

Independence of the hands is developed through the large number of pieces using contrapuntal devices. The simplest examples are **22** and **23**, in which imitation and inversion are first introduced, while **145a** and **b** provide the culminating example, for these two pieces may be played simultaneously on two pianos, the one being an inversion of the other.

* See article 'The So-called Bulgarian Rhythm' in *Béla Bartók Essays*, ed. B. Suchoff, Faber and Faber.

Examples of Bulgarian Rhythms in Mikrokosmos

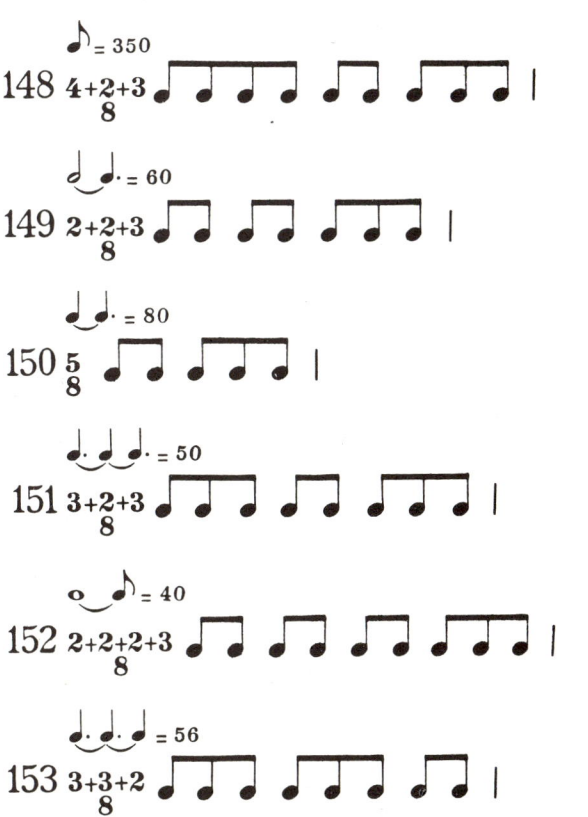

Independent phrasing appears in **26**, and **38** provides the first instance of playing *legato* against *staccato*. Apart from **40** and **41**, the left hand is never subordinate to the right hand, a common fault in music for beginners. Typical of Bartók's insistence on the equal development of the hands is **42**, in which right and left hands have different dynamic markings for the first time and characteristically change roles halfway through the piece.

Another unusual feature of *Mikrokosmos* is the large number of pieces based on a closed hand position, that is with the five fingers of each hand lying over five adjacent notes. Monotony is avoided by placing the hands at various distances from one another, by using contrary as well as parallel movement and by employing irregular phrase lengths, different rhythms and a variety of scales and modes.

Bartók does not require the thumb to be turned under until **98**, this landmark being stressed by the title *Thumbs Under*. However, lateral or sideways movement of the whole hand is required as early as **8**, and this technique is developed throughout the series. If the flexibility of the thumb is neglected, a compensatory feature is the development of strength in each finger equally. The fifth finger, so neglected in conventional scale and arpeggio practice, has to work hard in *Mikrokosmos*, and from as early as **10** it is required to play a black note, a deliberate ploy to ensure that the hand of the beginner is kept in a good position, with the fingers well over the keys.

There are many pieces at every level requiring the expansion and contraction of the hands from a five-finger position. A few pieces introduce hand crossing and many require the interlocking of hands.

The technique of chord playing is built up gradually from Volume 3 onwards through pieces concentrating on particular chords, such as **67**, **69**, **71**, **73**, **120**, **131**, and **144**. For **67** and **69** there are useful preliminary exercises in the Appendix, and in the Preface Bartók also suggests a way of simplifying the accompaniment of **69**, a procedure which encourages the pupil to 'take hold' of chords. Preparation for octave playing is provided in **112**, where the use of Bartók's fingering for the theme (1 + 2 in each hand) will ensure that wrists are in the correct physical condition for playing the sixths in the following variations, and octaves in later pieces.

Pedalling

There are two excellent preliminary exercises for the use of the sustaining pedal in the Appendix to Volume 2, and these should be studied before **47**, in which the use of the pedal is first required. In **47** the pedal is used to add colour and excitement to the musical portrayal of a *County Fair*, and this is typical of Bartók's unconventional attitude to the pedal. He seldom uses it to sustain *legato* melodies or to join chords. The most traditional use of the pedal is in **97**, a *Nocturne* reminiscent of Scriabin, and the most impressionistic in **144**, reminiscent of Debussy. Unusual tone colours are produced by the half-pedalling effects in **110** and **140**. The use of the *sostenuto* pedal (marked *prol. ped.*) is called for in **109**, and is desirable in **107** and **153**, but if it is not available fingers may be replaced silently on the relevant notes or chords to produce a similar effect.

The sustaining pedal adds to the remarkable effects of *Harmonics* in **102**. Here Bartók demonstrates his acute ear for pianistic tone-colour as he provides a folk-like melody with a shimmering background, produced by holding down certain notes without allowing them to sound.

The use of *una corda* is not specified anywhere in *Mikrokosmos*, nor indeed in any of Bartók's piano works. Peter Bartók recalls that his father expected him, as a young pupil, to produce soft tone by finger control alone. György Sándor, the eminent pianist who was a pupil of Bartók for four years, explains that using *una corda* was, in Bartók's opinion, a means of varying the quantity, but not the quality of tone, and so there was no need to specify its use.

Development of Musicianship

In his Preface to *Mikrokosmos* Bartók makes a number of important suggestions designed to develop the musicianship of pupils. He recommends transposition of the simpler pieces and exercises into other keys. This procedure is facilitated by the large number of pieces in a five-finger position, for once the pupil has found the new position for his hands, he can concentrate on the aural aspect of transposition.

Transcriptions, with octave-doubling, and more adventurous modifications such as playing accompaniment patterns as chords, are also suggested to test 'the more resourceful students' ingenuity'.

Throughout *Mikrokosmos* there are opportunities for ensemble work, in which musicianship is developed through a stimulating and enjoyable activity. As Bartók points out, 'It is important that students begin ensemble-playing at the earliest possible stage'. He gives practical suggestions for ensemble activities using one or two pianos, and encourages the resourceful teacher to make further experiments on similar lines.

A Textbook for Composers

Mikrokosmos is not merely a collection of graded teaching pieces in a new style, it is also a valuable compendium of compositional procedures and is still unsurpassed as a survey of twentieth century pianism. Bartók held that it was impossible to teach composition, and, typically, he declined to do so even when under financial pressure during his final years in America. However, like Bach, who in the preface to his *Inventions* declared that the purpose of his pieces was not only that students should learn to play with good style but also that they should 'acquire a taste for composition', Bartók provides pupils with models in composition.

To take but one example, the melody in the right hand of **12** is exactly reflected in the left hand. Once a pupil has discovered that the 'water-line' note is D, he can make up his own *Reflection* piece.

Lutoslawski has said that studying the works of Bartók 'has been one of the fundamerntal lessons to be taken by the majority of composers of my generation'. For older pupils a detailed analysis of the pieces in *Mikrokosmos* would provide a unique textbook of compositional techniques, while for many listeners such analysis would enhance their enjoyment of Bartók's music.

Why Use Mikrokosmos?

Skill-learning depends for its success on a systematic structure and this is provided in *Mikrokosmos*. The main elements of piano technique are covered, with a variety of material at each level to allow for choice. Bartók introduces one new difficulty at a time in a logical sequence, and he provides for consolidation and revision in a spiral of progression. The orderly presentation of technical and theoretical material is allied to a systematic increase in the difficulties of interpretation.

The journey through Bartók's 'Little World' is ideally started in childhood, but older students will benefit from the logical sequence of technical training. They will find nothing to insult the intelligence and much to stimulate the imagination. Advanced students who have had only a traditional training will find in *Mikrokosmos* an ideal introduction to the techniques necessary for the performance of much contemporary music, and students at all levels will benefit from using the pieces in *Mikrokosmos* as sight-reading material.

Accurate observation and a high degree of concentration are required for successful performance of these pieces, but because they are short the satisfaction of mastering them can be obtained quickly.

Mikrokosmos provides intriguing technical and imaginative challenges to pupils of all ages. The pieces cover a wide range, from peasant vigour to aristocratic poise, from gentle humour to dynamic excitement, from grave thoughtfulness to fervent passion.

In *Mikrokosmos* technique and aesthetics are reconciled far more successfully than in most pedagogical works. The unfailing inventiveness of Bartók is shown particularly well in the variety of two-part textures in the early pieces. Even the shortest pieces are never trivial. As a poet condenses his ideas into few words, so Bartók condenses his musical ideas to produce the miniature masterpieces of *Mikrokosmos*.

Nevertheless, *Mikrokosmos* is a *little* world and should be supplemented if pupils are to be equipped to play, for example, pieces employing a *bel canto* style, such as Chopin's *Nocturnes*. In Bartók's uncompromising view, the piano is at its most expressive not when imitating a vocal style but when being true to its own nature, a percussion instrument. So, although there are opportunities in *Mikrokosmos* for pupils to practise the deception that the piano can produce a singing *legato*, further material, such as Schumann's *Album for the Young*, should also be studied.

The many ternary structures in *Mikrokosmos* help the pupil to appreciate the importance of repetition and symmetry, but as there are no pieces in sonata form sonatinas by Clementi and Beethoven and the easier sonatas of Mozart should be introduced at an appropriate stage so that the pupil obtains an understanding of this form.

Mikrokosmos includes material which enables the teacher to provide enlightened instruction in the theoretical aspects of music, efficient training in the manual skills required for playing the piano and, above all, a means to awaken the pupil's aesthetic appreciation and deepen his musical understanding. In *Mikrokosmos* we have a bird's-eye view of the larger world of Bartók's creative output, itself a synthesis of elements from the past, from folk music and from contemporary techniques. So *Mikrokosmos* provides a key not only to Bartók's world, but to the world of twentieth century music.

In *Mikrokosmos* the combined experience of Bartók the pianist, Bartók the composer, Bartók the folk music specialist and Bartók the teacher are united to produce pieces which will ensure that those who study them will have a well developed technique, a fine awareness of tone colour, an understanding of the structure of music and a broad musical outlook.

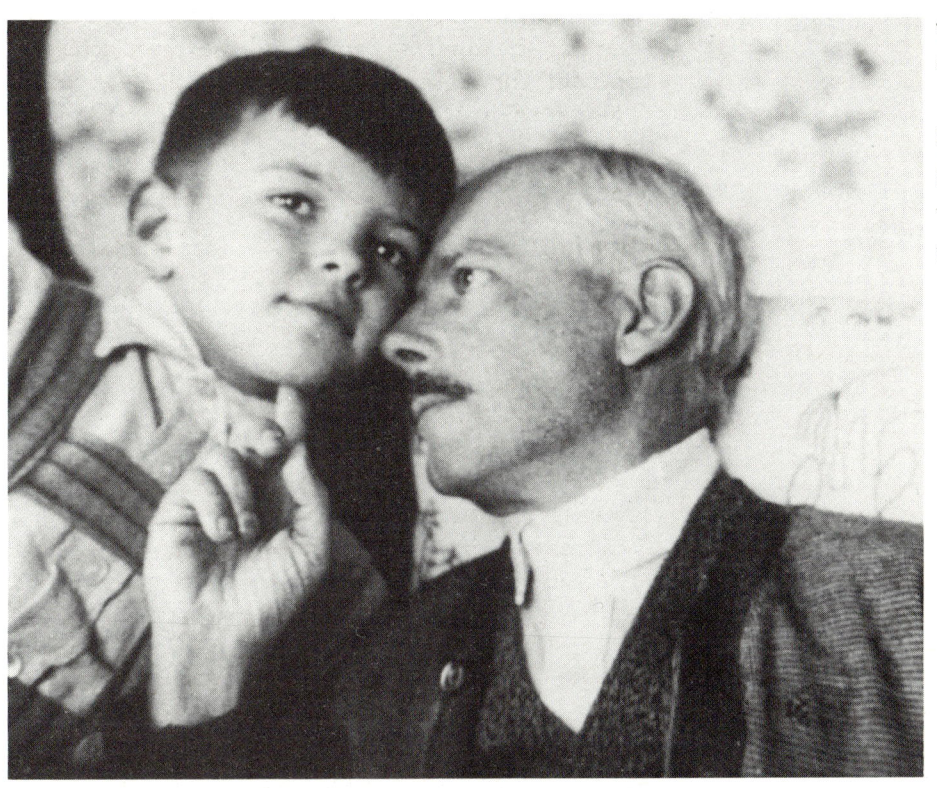

Photo by Ditta Pásztory-Bartók

The composer with his son Peter (reproduced by courtesy of Peter Bartók)

Publisher's Note

Belá Bartók had worked on and off since the 1920s on the pieces eventually to become Mikrokosmos. Teaching his son Peter (from about 1933 on) inspired many of the easier pieces. These eventually formed Volumes 1 and 2, which he dedicated to Peter (see the last music-page in each volume). The Six Dances in Bulgarian Rhythm which conclude the sixth volume were dedicated to the eminent English pianist Harriet Cohen (1895-1967).

The first edition of the six volumes of Mikrokosmos was published by Boosey & Hawkes in London and New York on 16 April 1940, the composer having completed his MS. in 1939. Work on publication was, of course, carried out against the background of international tension and dislocation of the early months of World War II. Extant correspondence describes the problems experienced in mailing proofs to and from Hungary at this time.

It is a tribute both to the composer – expecting almost daily to leave his native country for the USA (the original intention was a concert-tour, and the journey did not begin until October 1940) – and the persistence of his publishers that the entire work was engraved, proof-read and printed between December 1939 and April 1940.

The original edition was published with three languages – English, French and Hungarian. In 1951, shortly after Boosey & Hawkes had established a post-war commercial base in the new Federal Republic of Germany, a revised edition substituting the Hungarian text with German was published. At the same time a Hungarian / German edition was issued under licence by the Hungarian State music publisher Zenemükiadó Vállalat (later Editio Musica Budapest). In the intervening period a number of textual corrections were made; in particular the French piece-titles underwent quite considerable revision.

In 1986 Boosey & Hawkes decided that this major work deserved a completely new edition. Peter Bartók, now the proprietor of the Bartók Archive in the USA, was approached about the project. He responded with enthusiasm, and with the assistance of a team of international experts arranged for the printed editions to be compared with the original manuscripts. It was also decided to restore the Hungarian text, thus fulfilling Béla Bartók's own plan to include *four* languages in the original edition; a plan clearly frustrated by the political circumstances of 1939 / 40.

The original music pages were retained, using the earliest 'clean' printed copies available of the first edition and further corrections inserted on to photographic reproductions by the staff engraver at Boosey & Hawkes, Mr R. A. White. The cover, headings and other texts were redesigned by the distinguished typographer Gerald Cinamon of the firm of Cinamon and Kitzinger.

It was also decided to retain the 6-volume format, though it was known that the composer originally favoured a 4-volume set. The publishers advised him at the time that this was not commercially practicable, and the same rationale was maintained when planning the 1987 edition.

Despite the speed with which the first edition was produced, there were in fact very few musical errors in the text. An important alteration in Volume 6 (no. 144) has been annotated in the Notes to the present edition.

With the exception of Béla Bartók's own Hungarian preface (to which the composer's name has now been restored) all other language texts have been revised and re-translated. Notable in this regard were the rather unsatisfactory English and French prefaces to the 1940 edition (and indeed the 1951 German preface) which omitted some important statements of emphasis that were evidently considered too advanced for the Western public.

Bartók at the time made some quite forcible objections when the publisher wished to insert some references to the 'modernity' of *Mikrokosmos*. He wrote (letter to the late Dr Ernst Roth, 9 January 1940):

'... If you as publisher want to prepare the public for the worse, you may publish [the proposed insertions] separately in a leaflet (if possible in pink or green) and put this *removable* leaflet into the 1. – 4. books, as a kind of advertisement, issued by the publisher, and not belonging to the publication.'

In the same letter he wrote:

'I would never ... make excuses for the "modernity" etc; besides I don't like the word "modern" at all! Think of it: in 20, or let us say in 40 years the work will cease to be modern. And what does it mean, "modern"? This word has no definite sens[e], can be misinterpreted, misunderstood."

47 years later, even though *Mikrokosmos* has become firmly established in the piano teaching repertoire, we can still marvel at the pristine freshness of Bartók's musical thought and ingenuity, which he expresses at the same time in the practical context of his *153 Progressive Piano Pieces*.

It is therefore with pleasure – indeed not without pride – that the publishers now present this new edition of *Mikrokosmos*.

Christine Brown

Christine Brown was born and educated in Leeds, Yorkshire. Having studied piano and viola at the Royal College of Music, London, to which she had gained a Foundation scholarship, she returned to the North of England.

After winning a YSO Concert Soloists' Competition, she developed a combined career as teacher and performer. Well-known through her teaching books and articles, she has lectured extensively to piano teachers in Britain and the USA. Other activities include recitals on the virginals, composing, accompanying and adjudicating.

Miss Brown has made a speciality of the study of Bartók's piano music, with particular emphasis on the composer's pedagogical compositions, notably, of course, his *Mikrokosmos*.

In this field, and particularly since 1977, she has lectured and written widely. Of major importance are her dissertation for a Master's degree at York University ('The pedagogical importance of Bartók's *Mikrokosmos*'); a lecture demonstration, 'Bartók's Music for the Young' (part of the centenary celebrations at Bretton Hall, Yorkshire, of Bartók's birth), a summer workshop lecture on *Mikrokosmos* at Dayton, Ohio, in 1983, and an illustrated lecture on Bartók's *For Children* at the EPTA International Conference in London in 1986.

In virtue of her extensive experience, Boosey & Hawkes has commissioned this extended essay from Christine Brown on *Mikrokosmos* in conjunction with the new, definitive edition of Bartók's masterpiece (1987) prepared under the supervision of Peter Bartók, second son of the composer, who has in turn contributed an introduction to the present booklet. The writer addresses the 'good, average piano teacher' in her perceptive and informed review of *Mikrokosmos*, which also includes a general background to the composer and his works for piano, especially his major contribution to the piano teaching repertoire.